I0478453

VOL.1
Ed.2

Gothicscopic

kaleidoscopes

coloring book

by

Tabz Jones

To see the full catalog of my work go to
www.gothictoggs.net

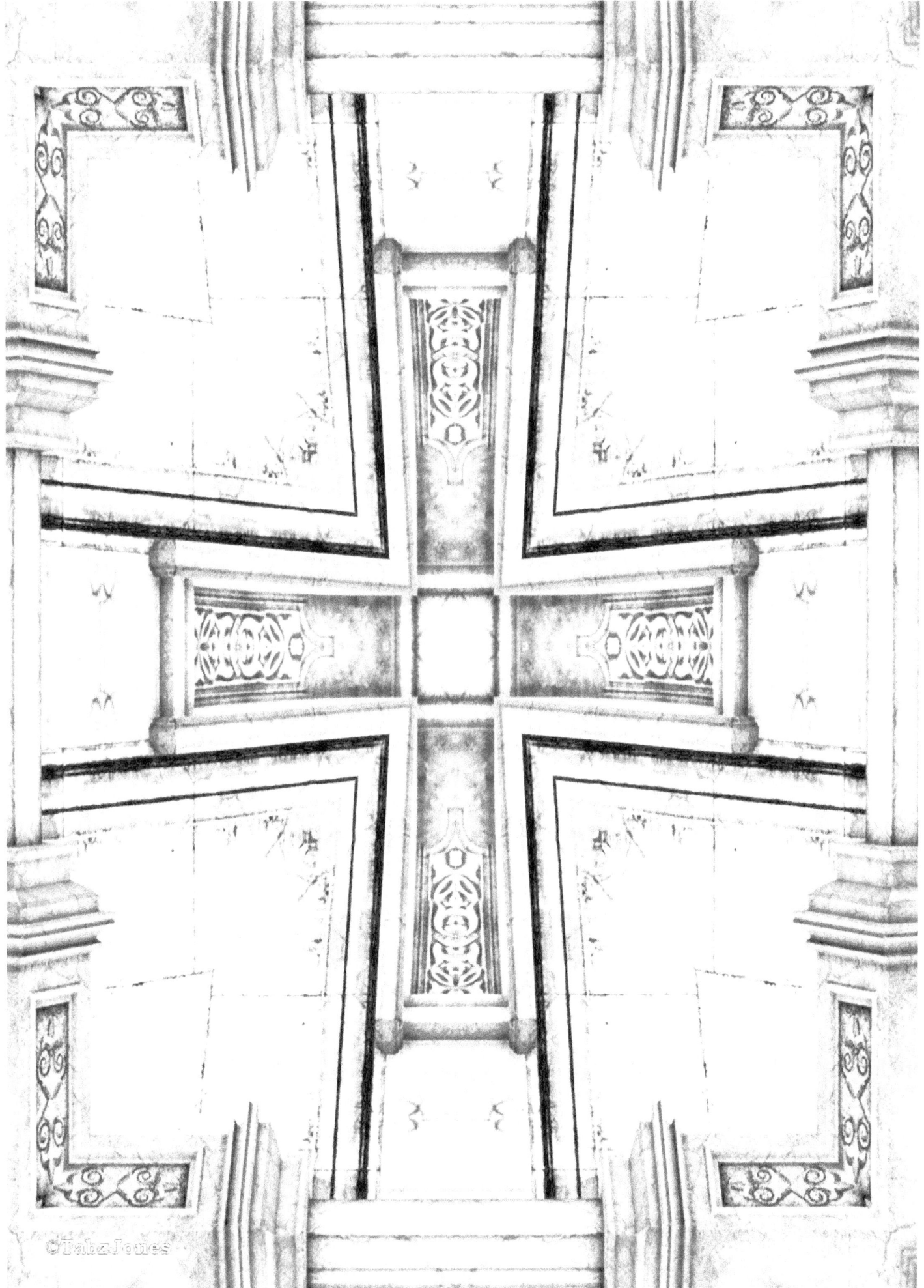

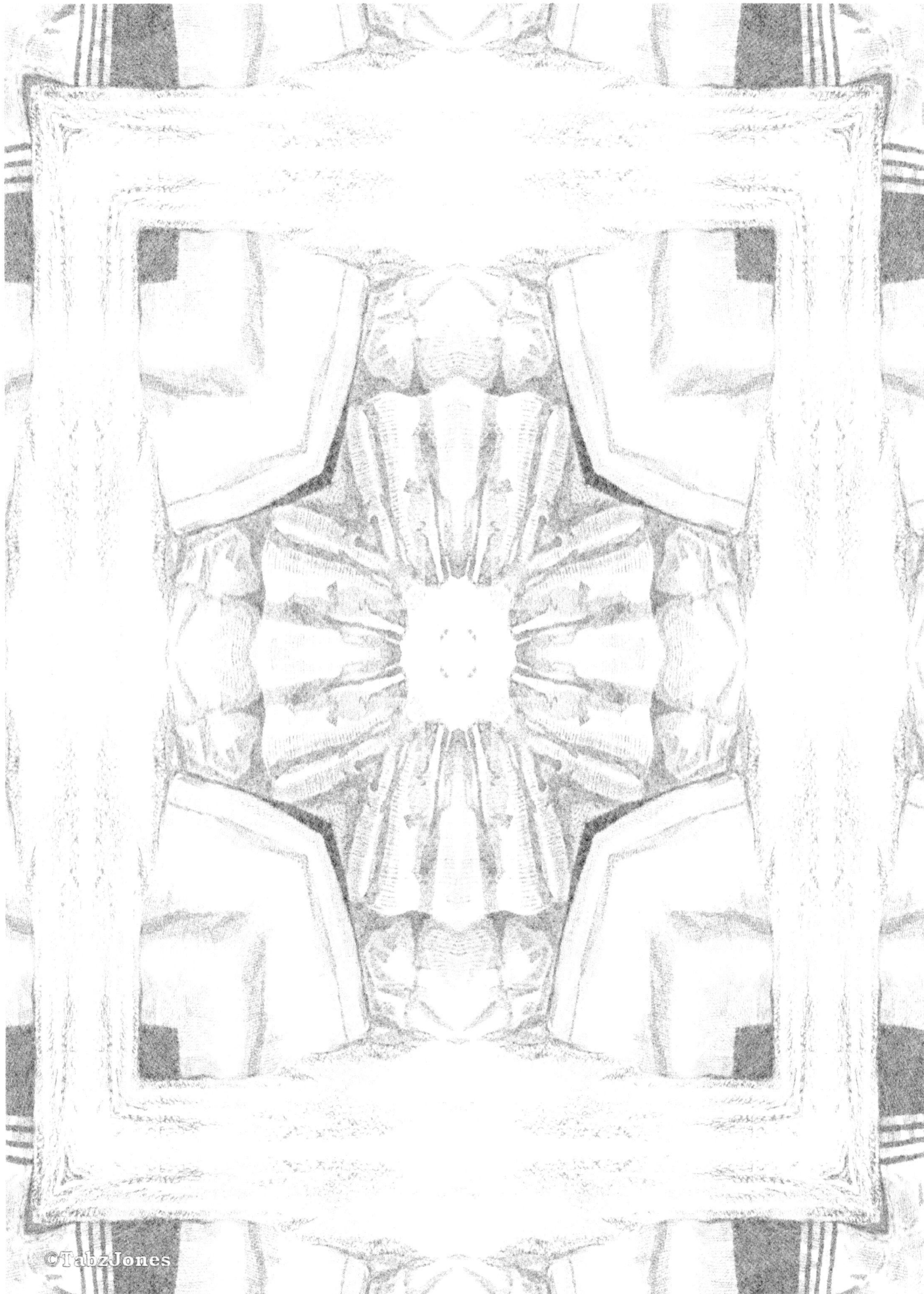

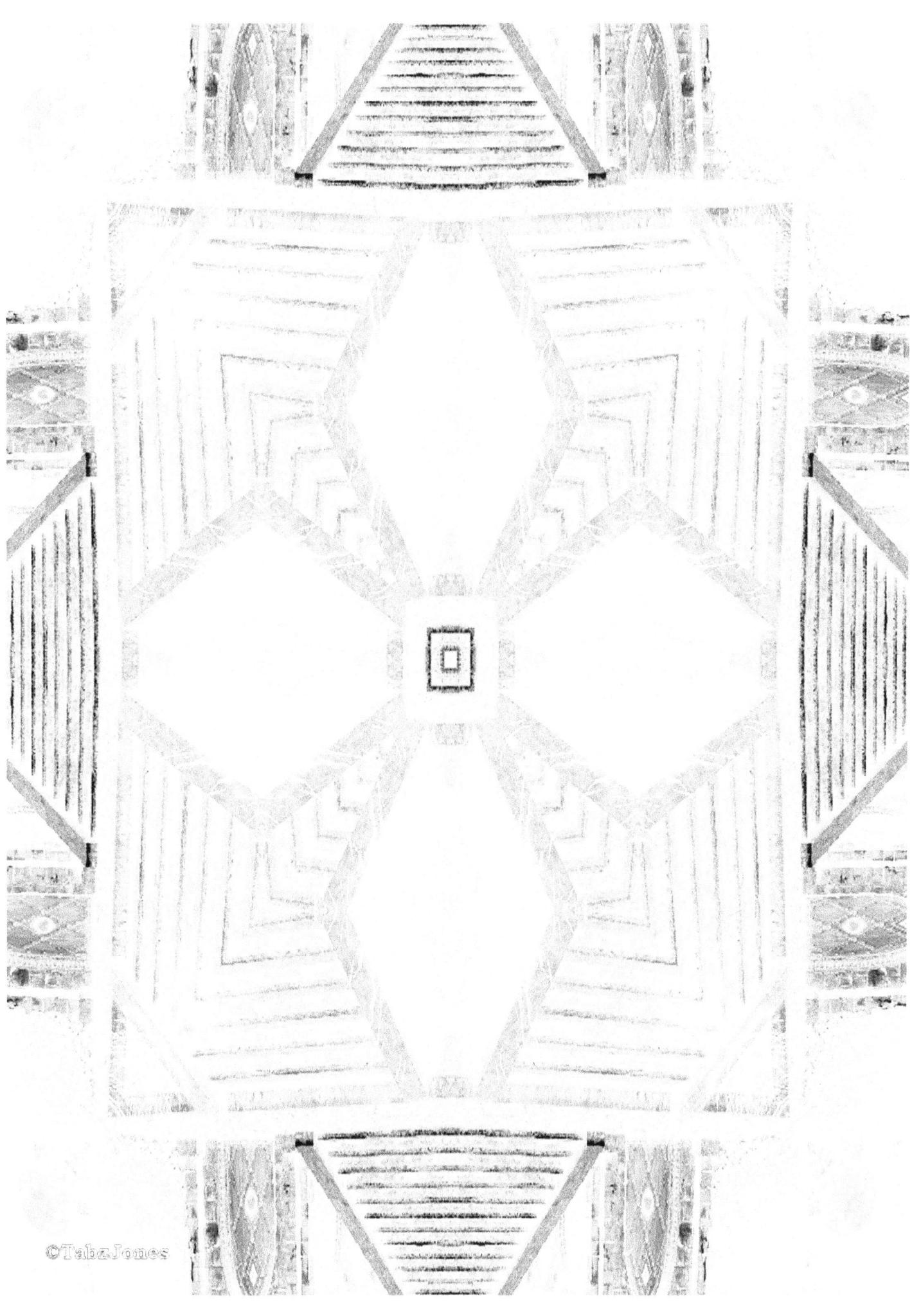
©TabzJones

©TabzJones

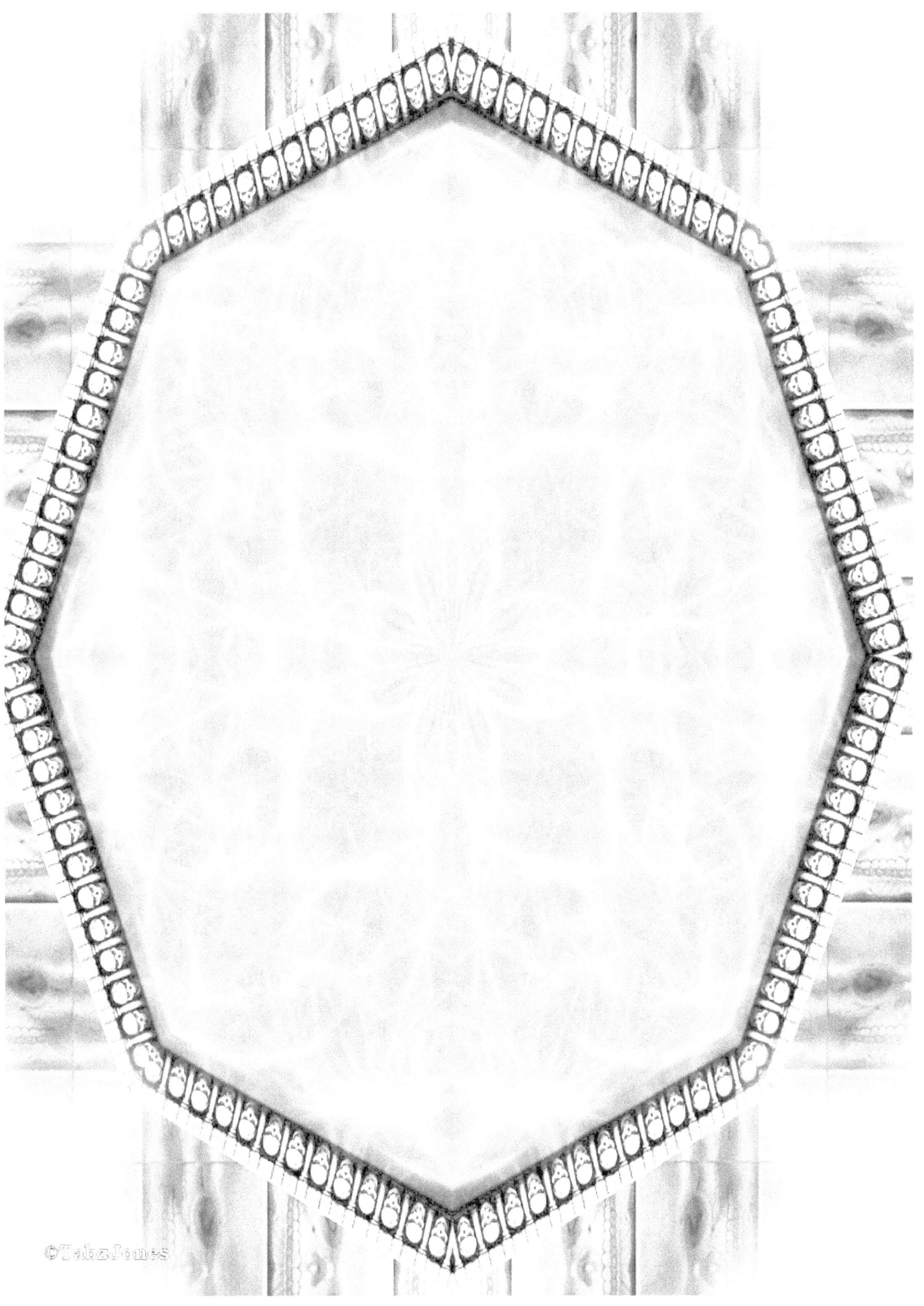

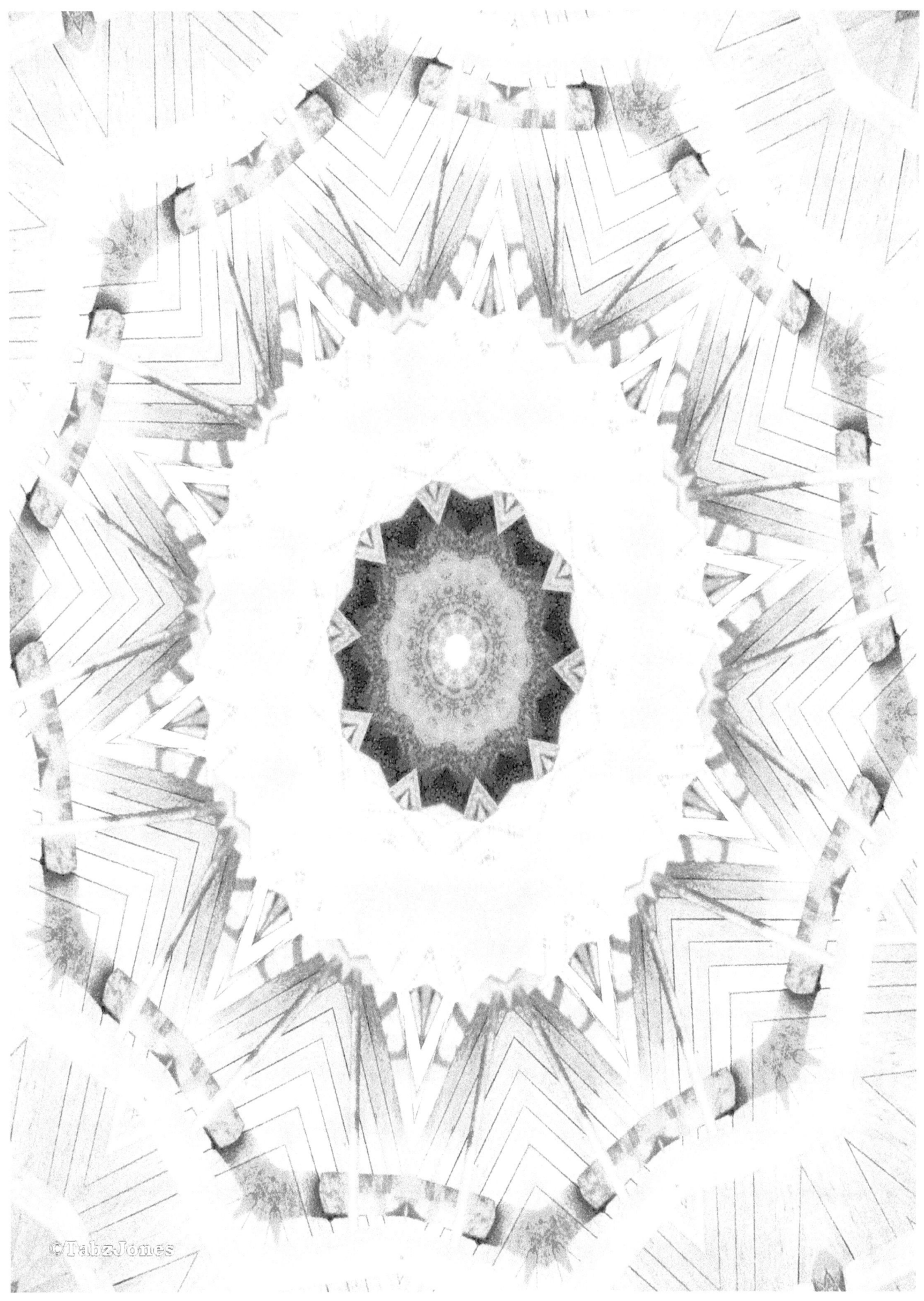

©TabzJones

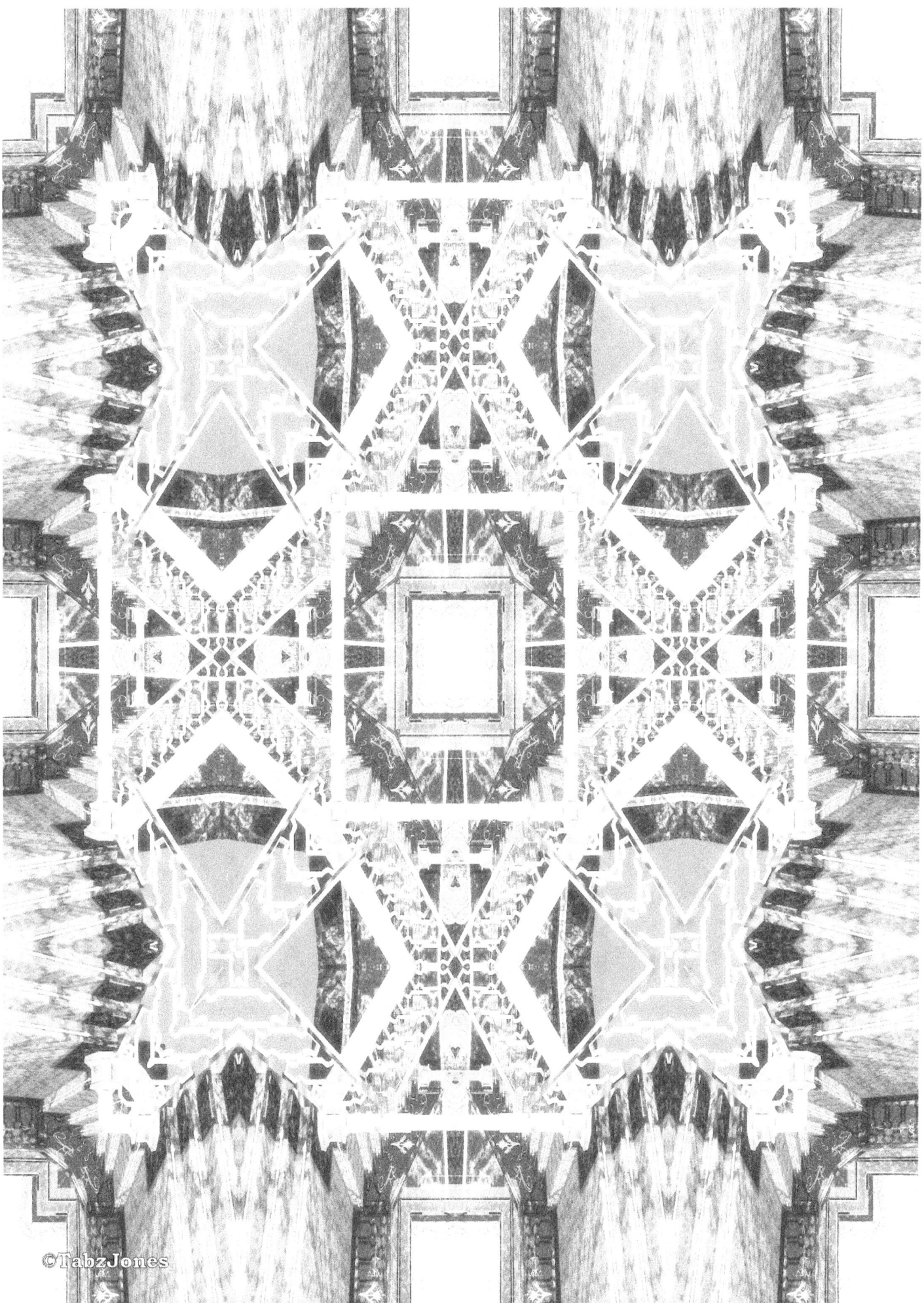
©TabzJones

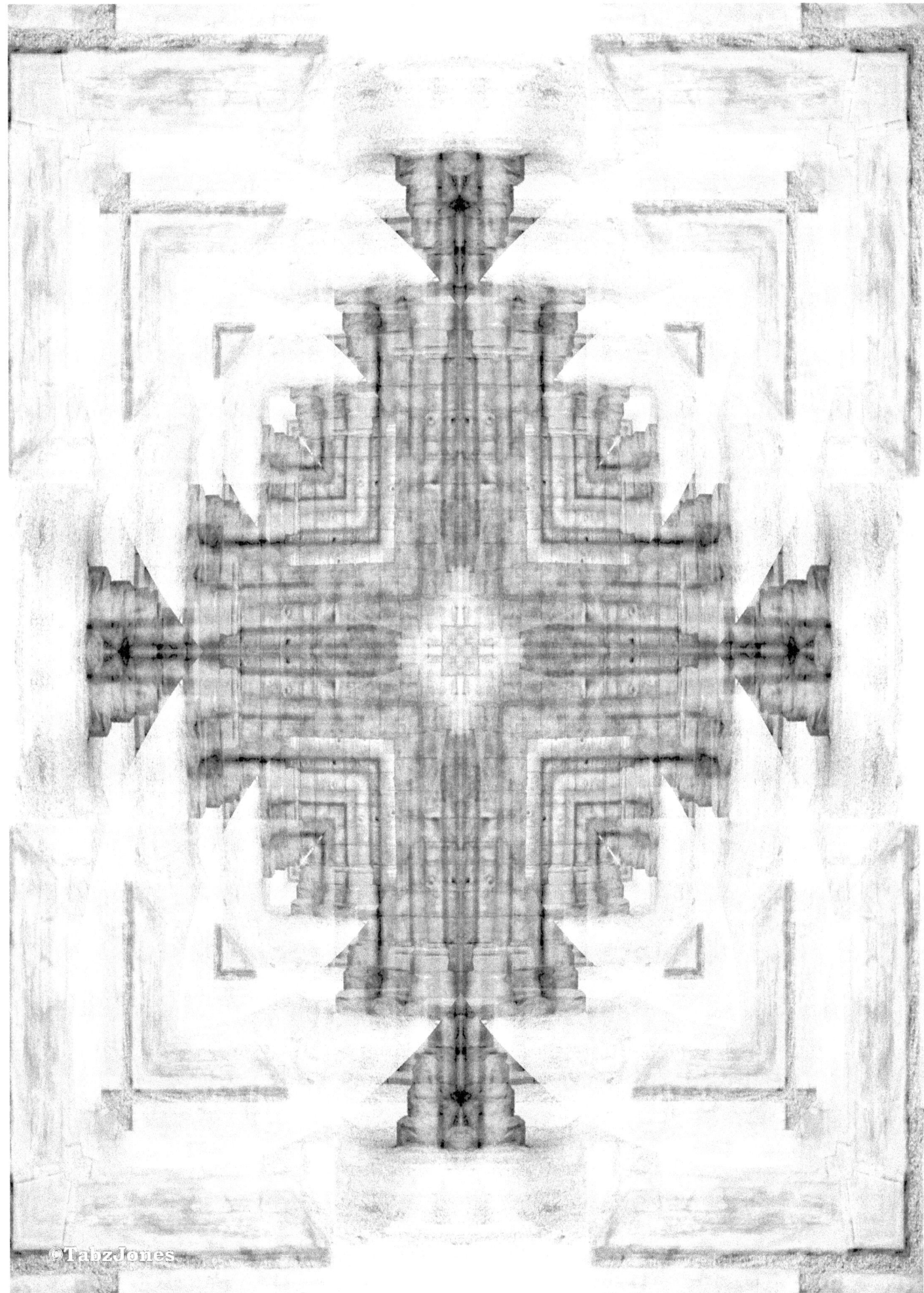
©TabzJones

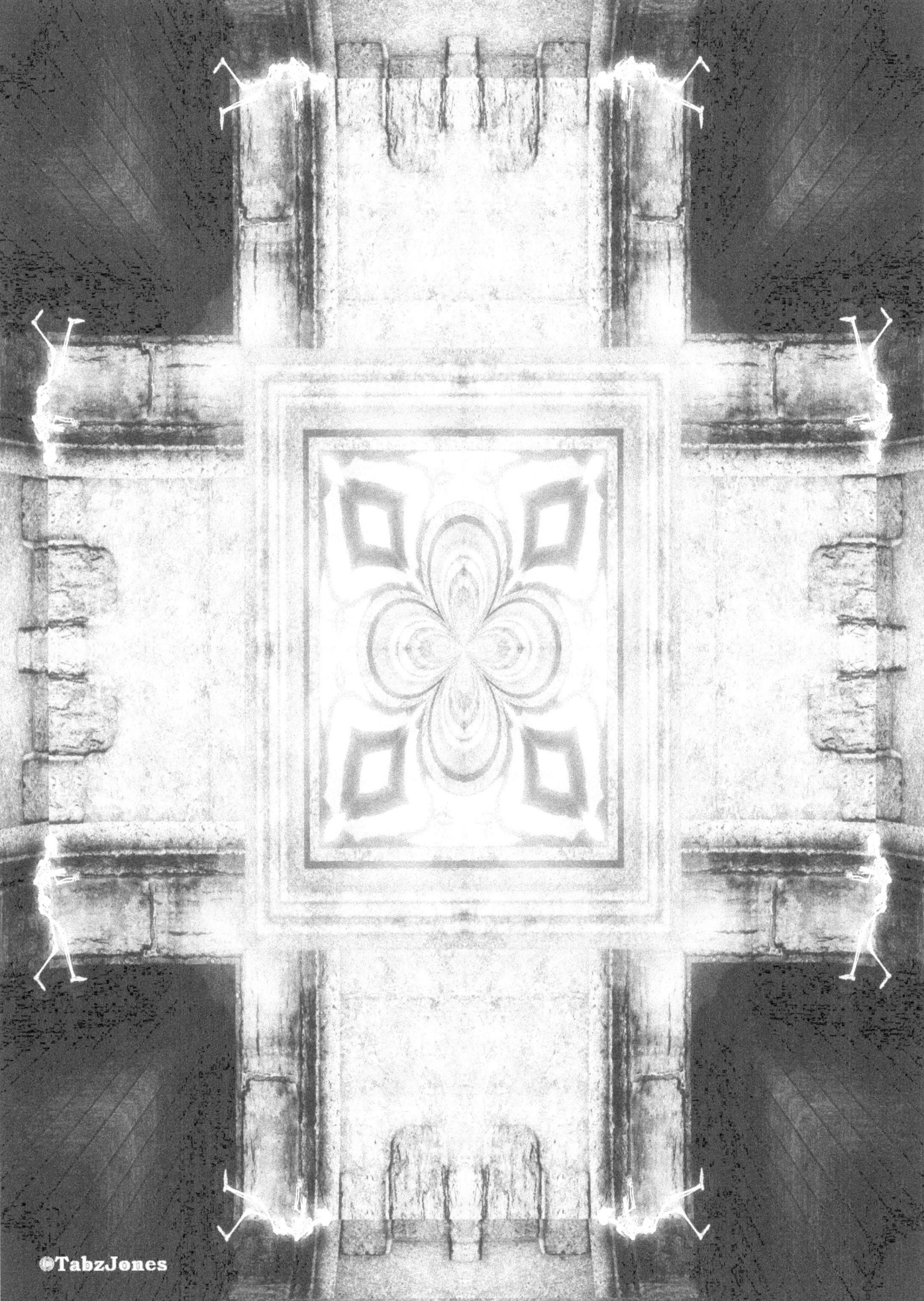

©TabzJones

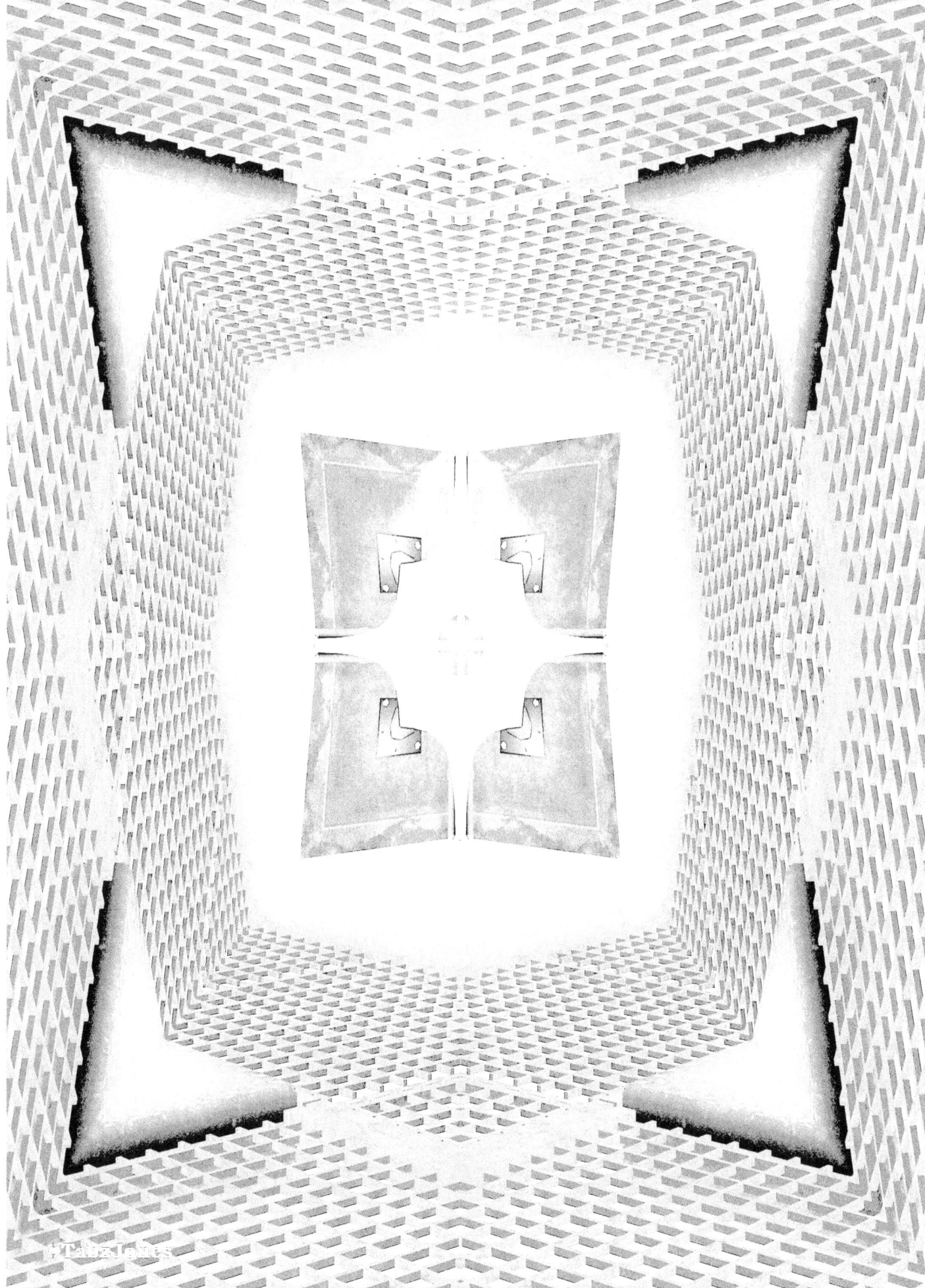

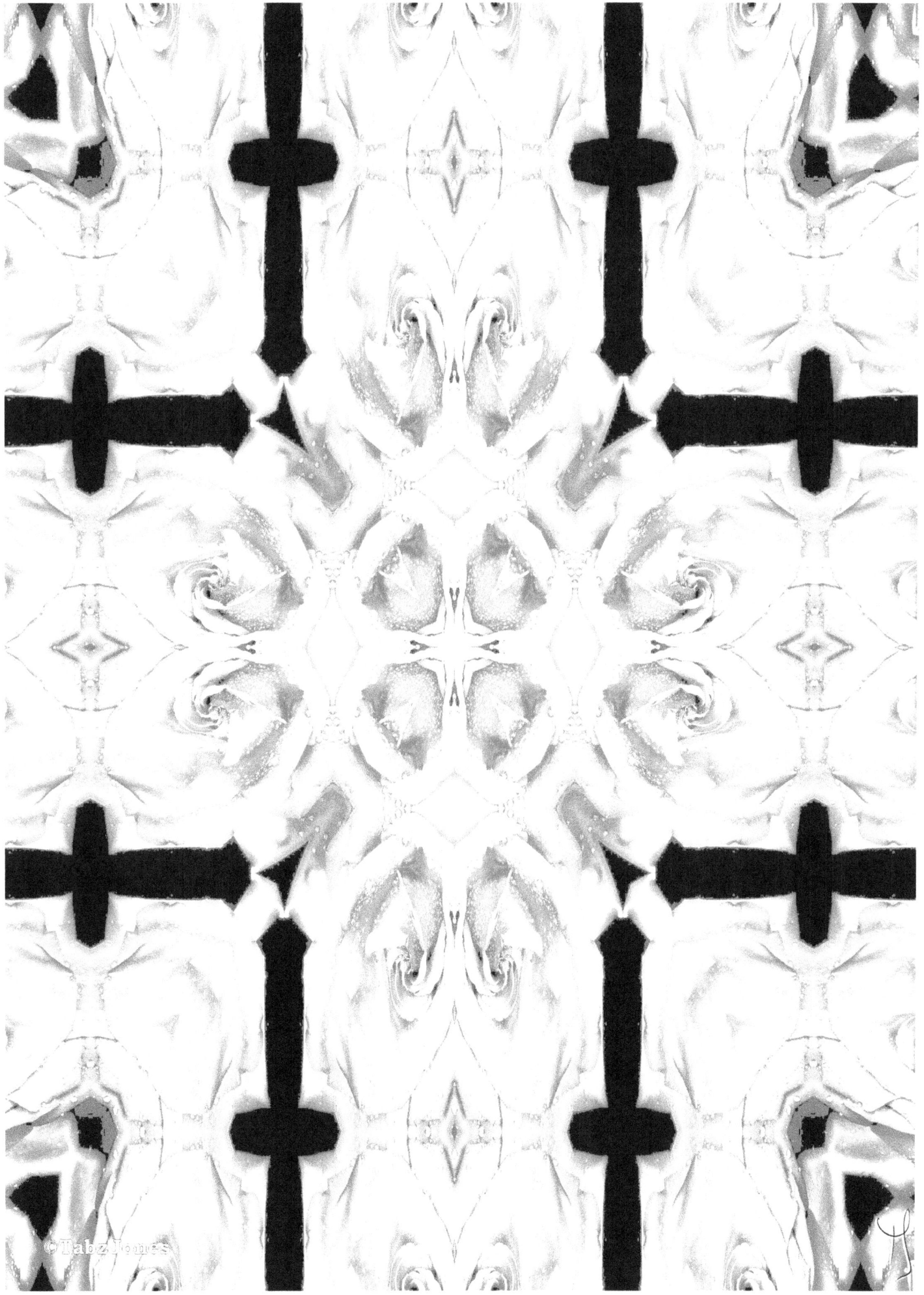

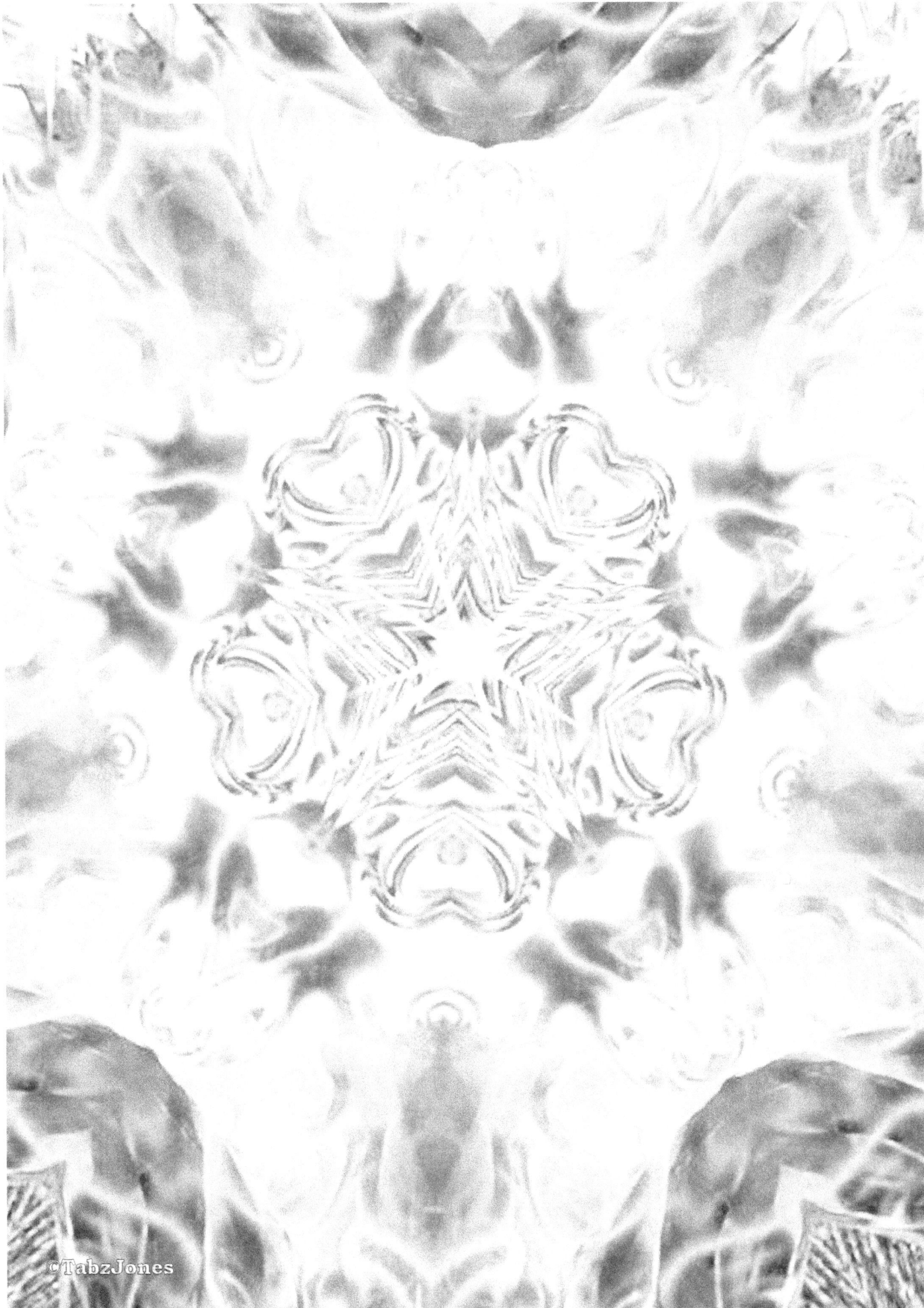

©TabzJones

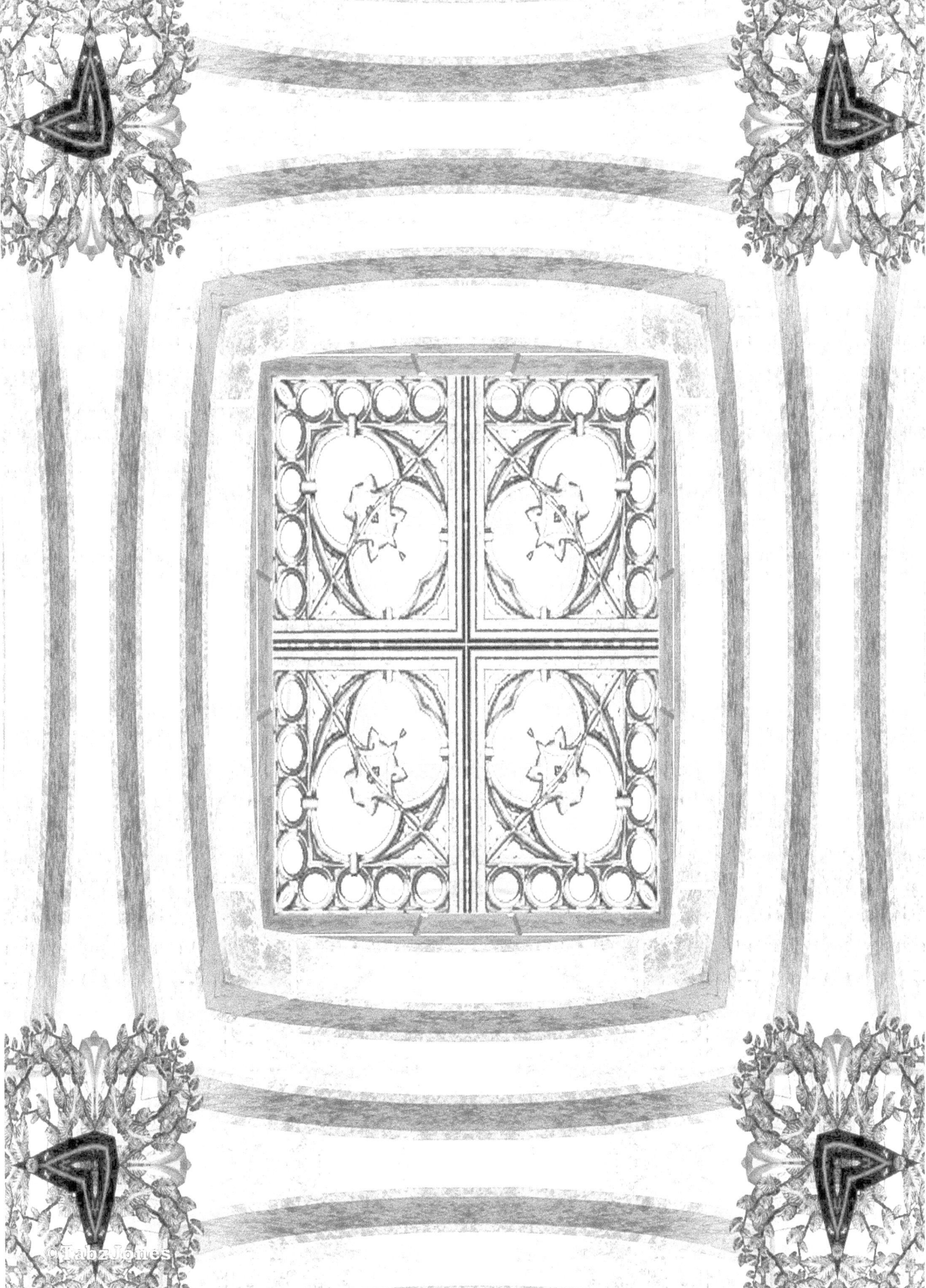

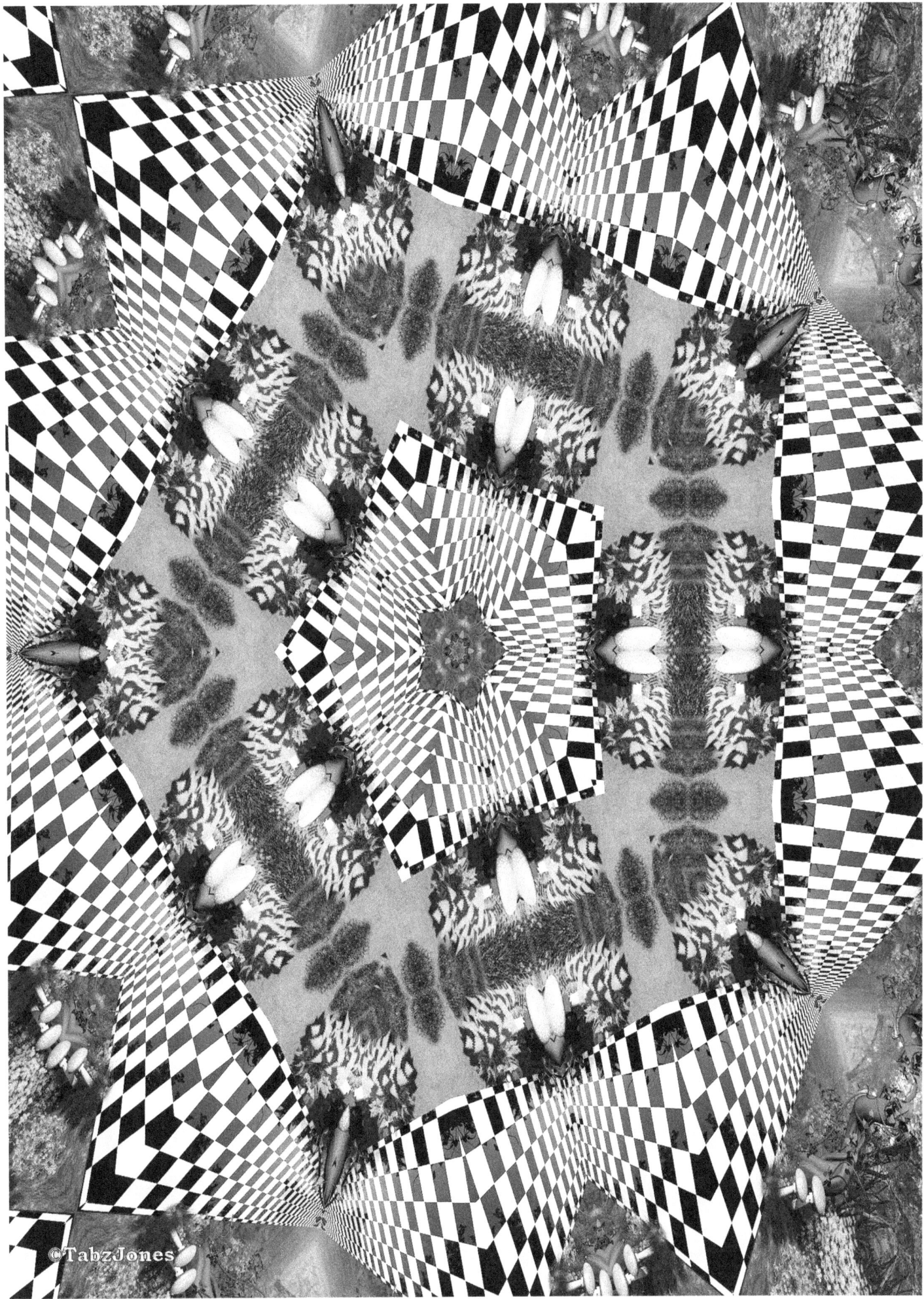
©TabzJones

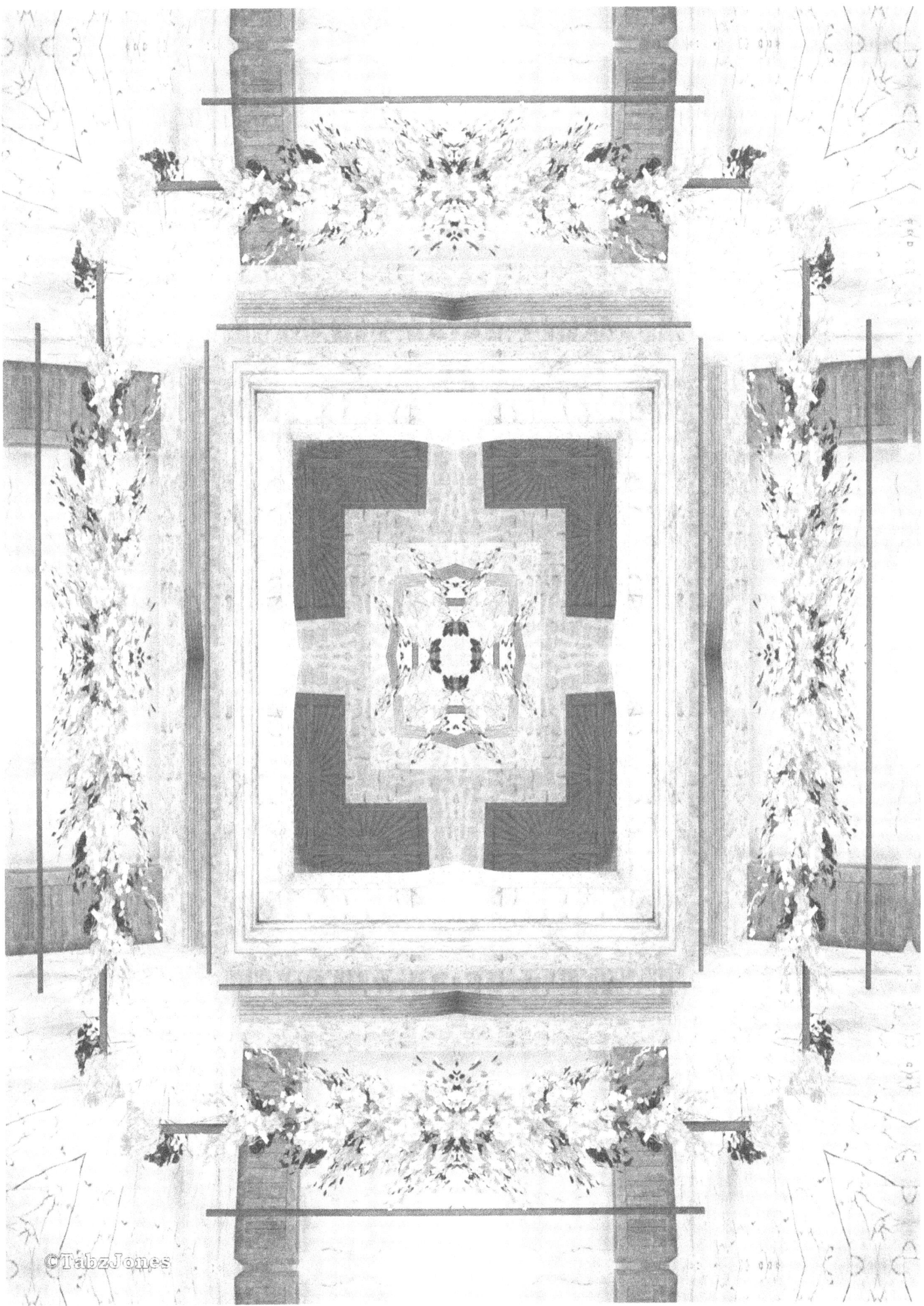

©TabzJones

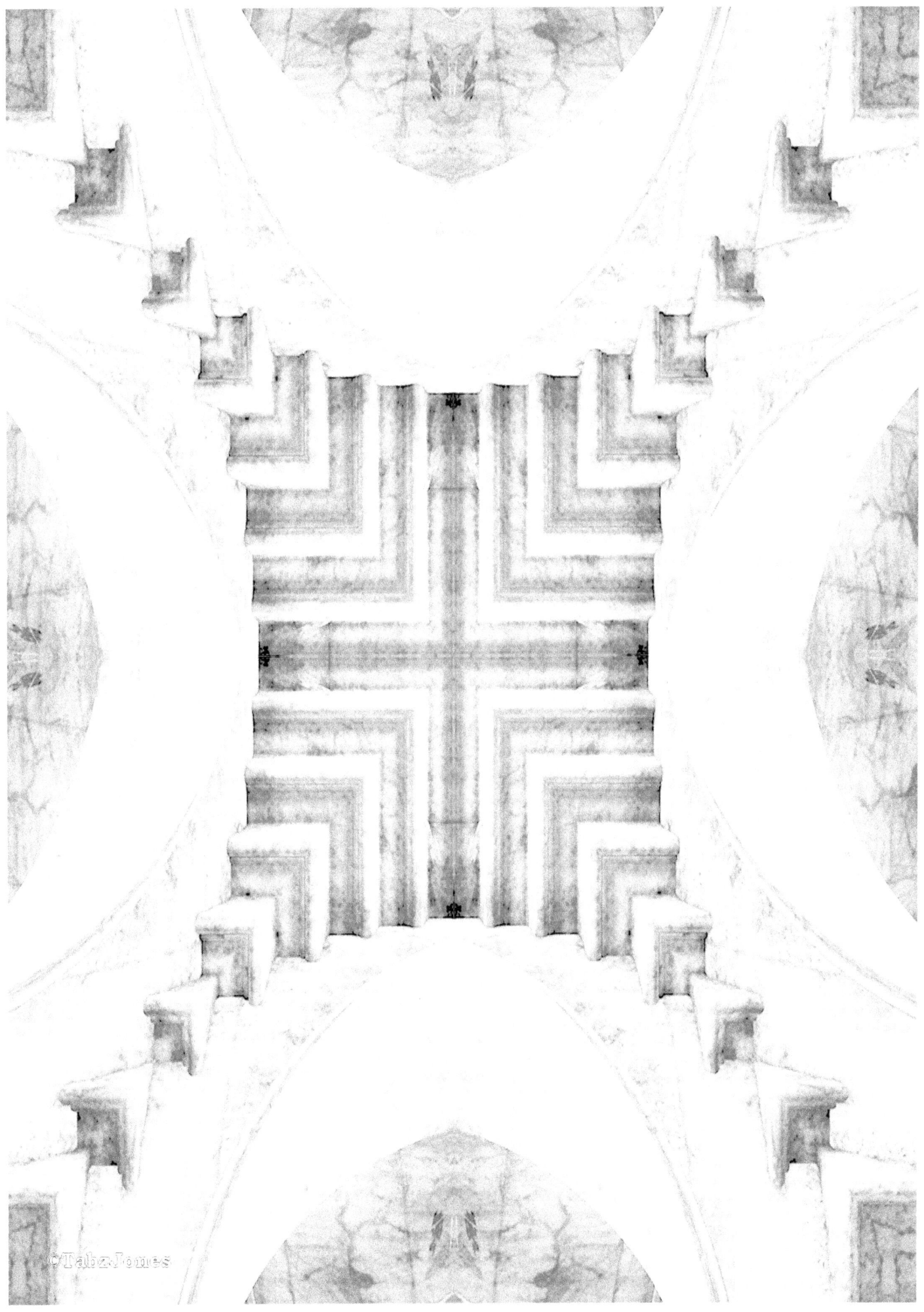

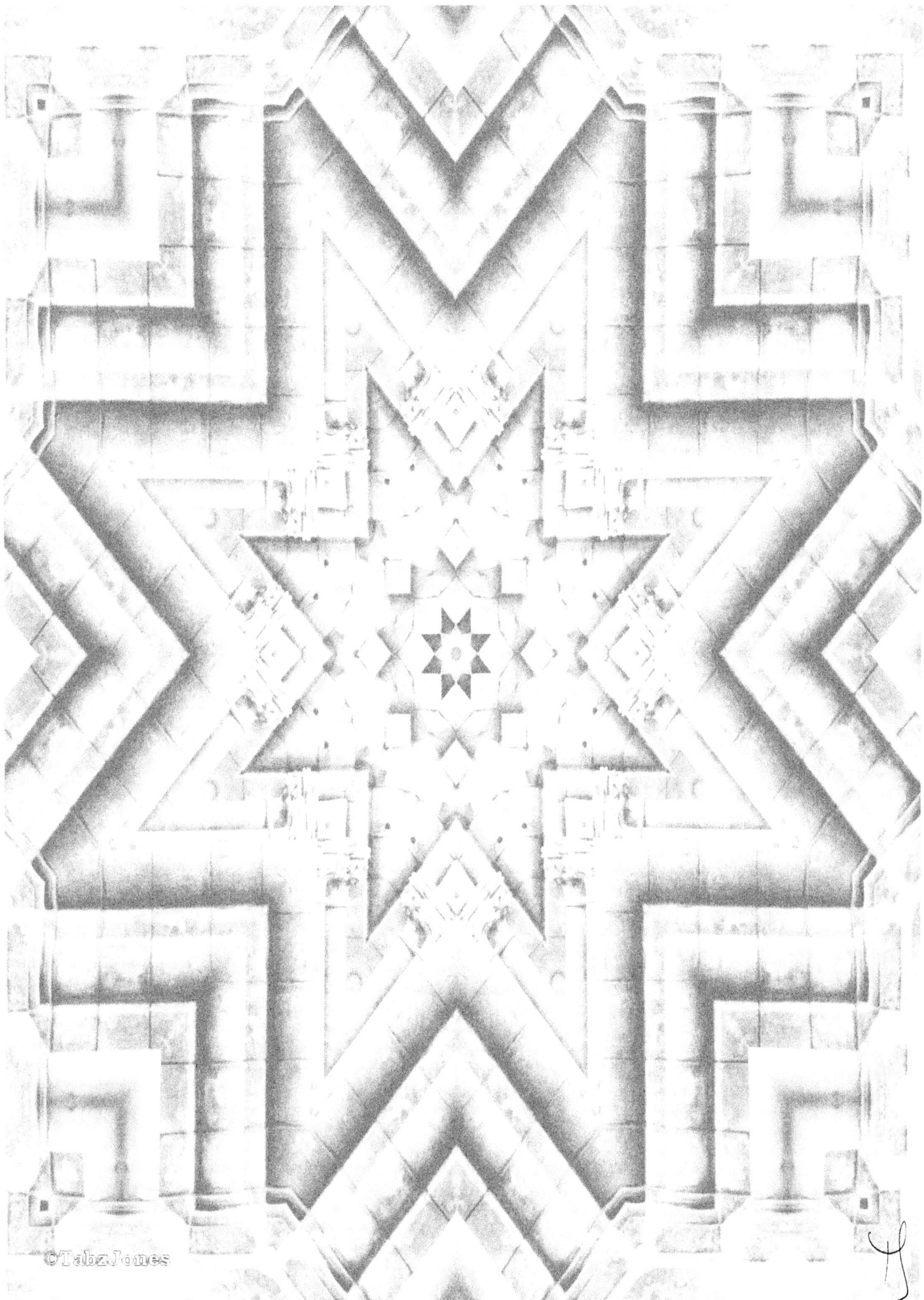

©TabzJones

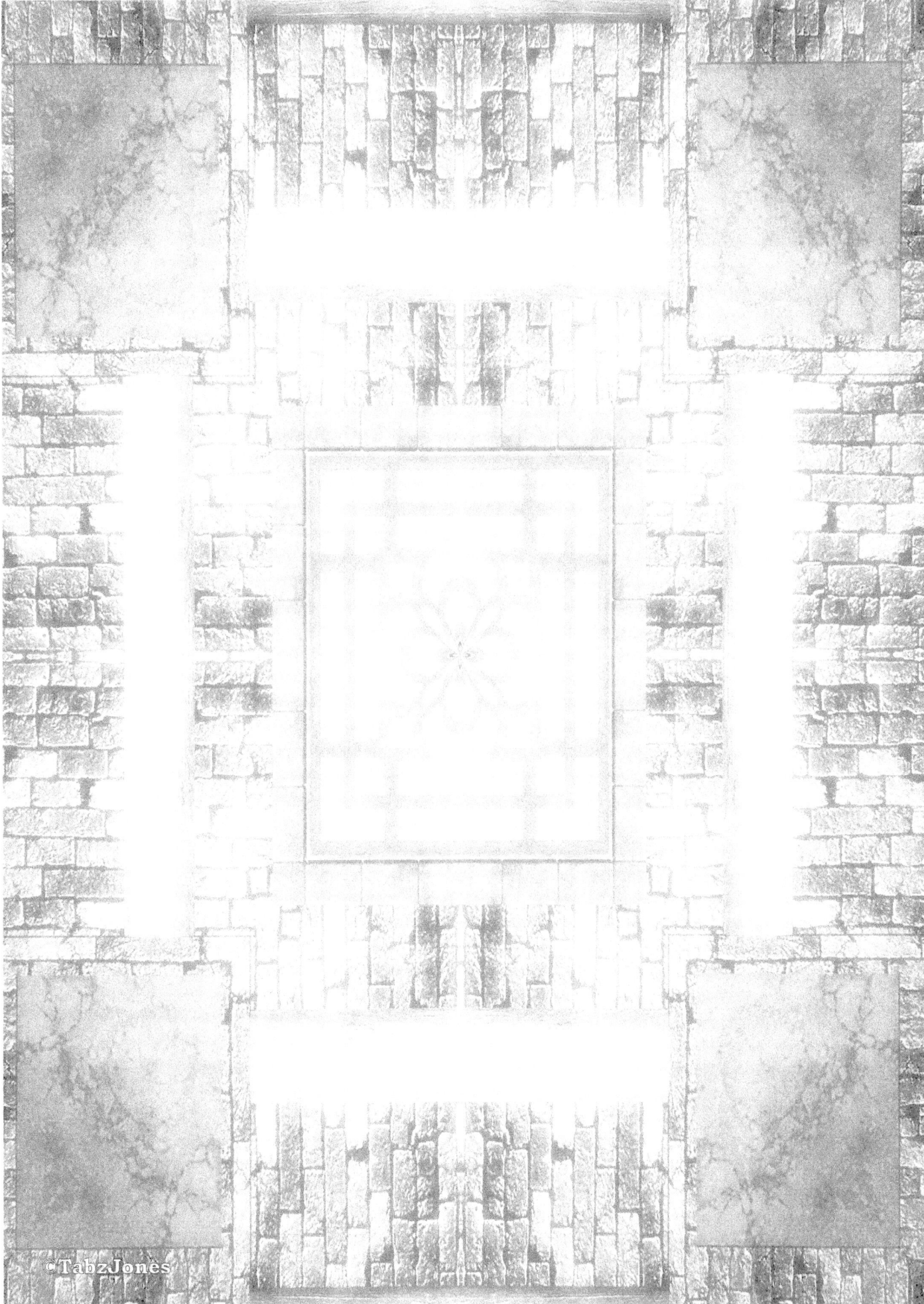

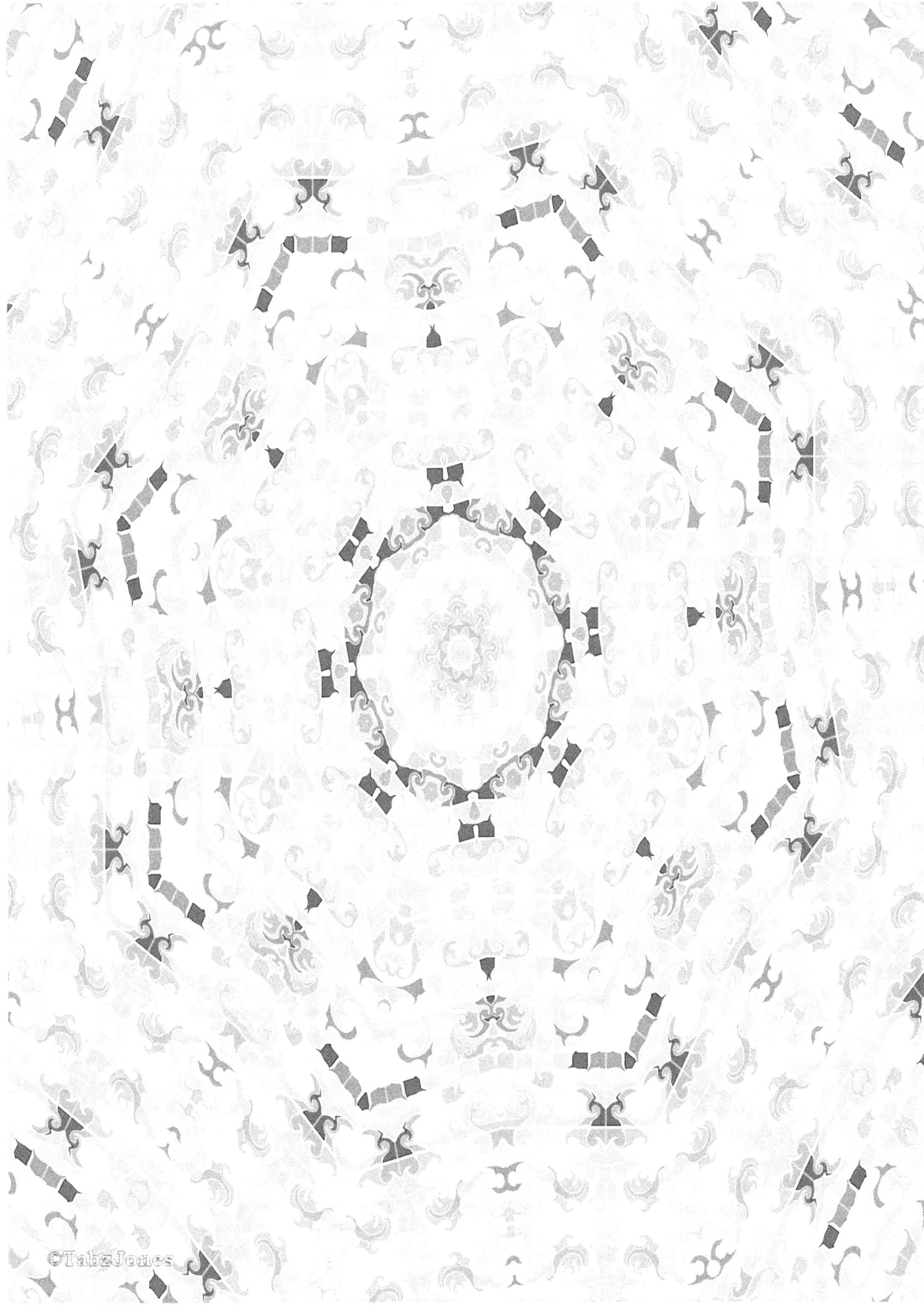

©TabzJones

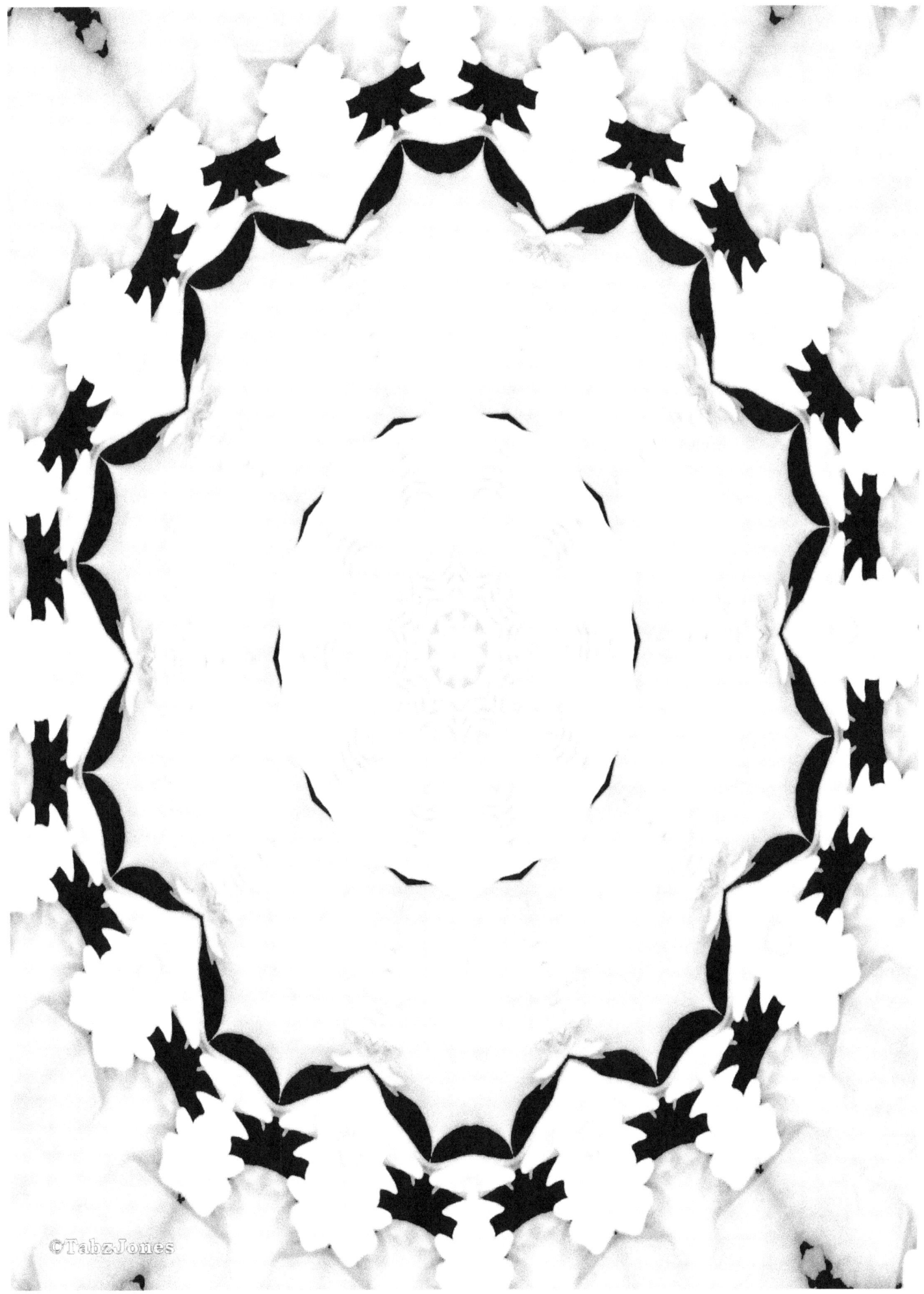

©TabzJones

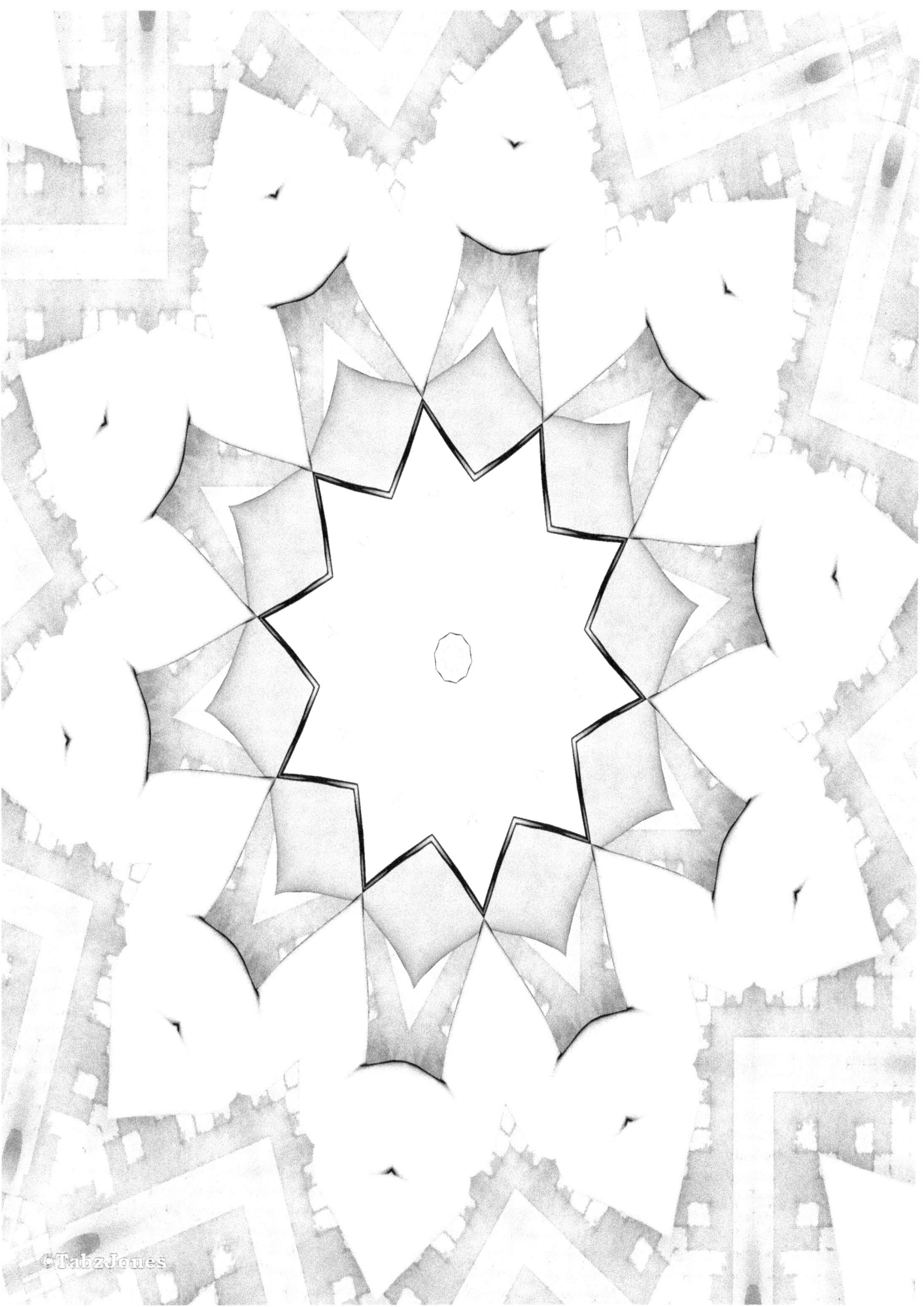

©TabzJones

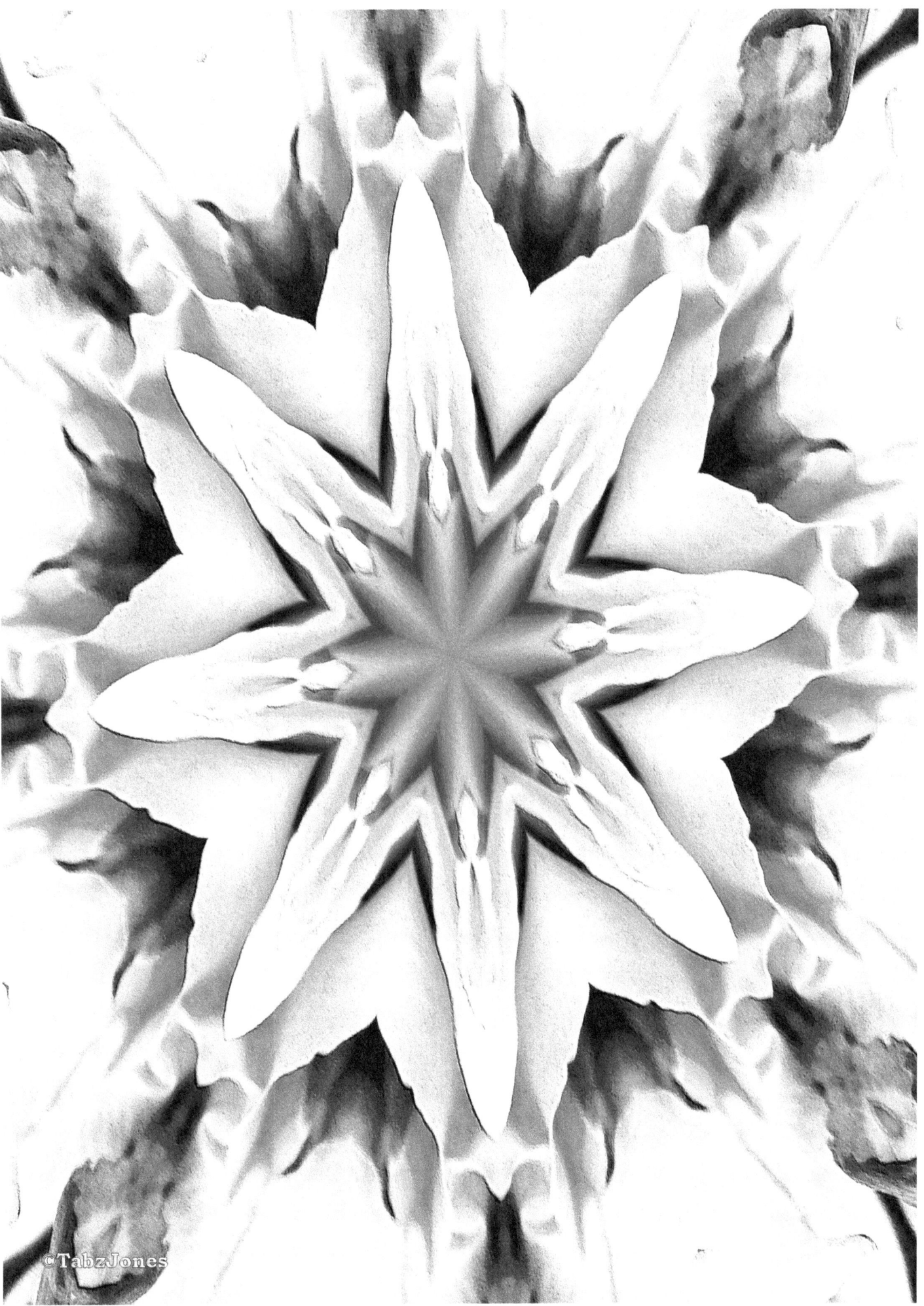

©TabzJones

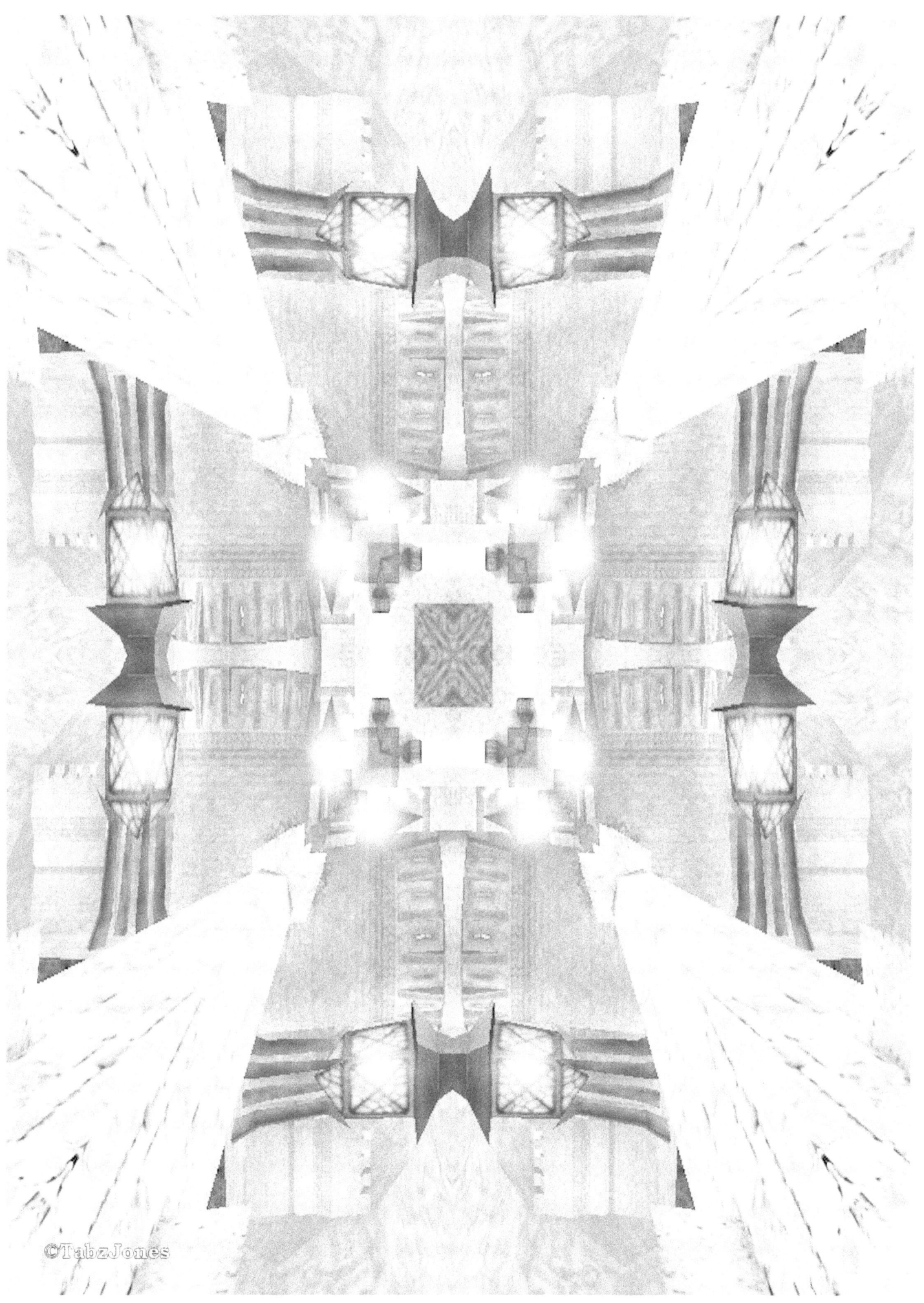

©TabzJones

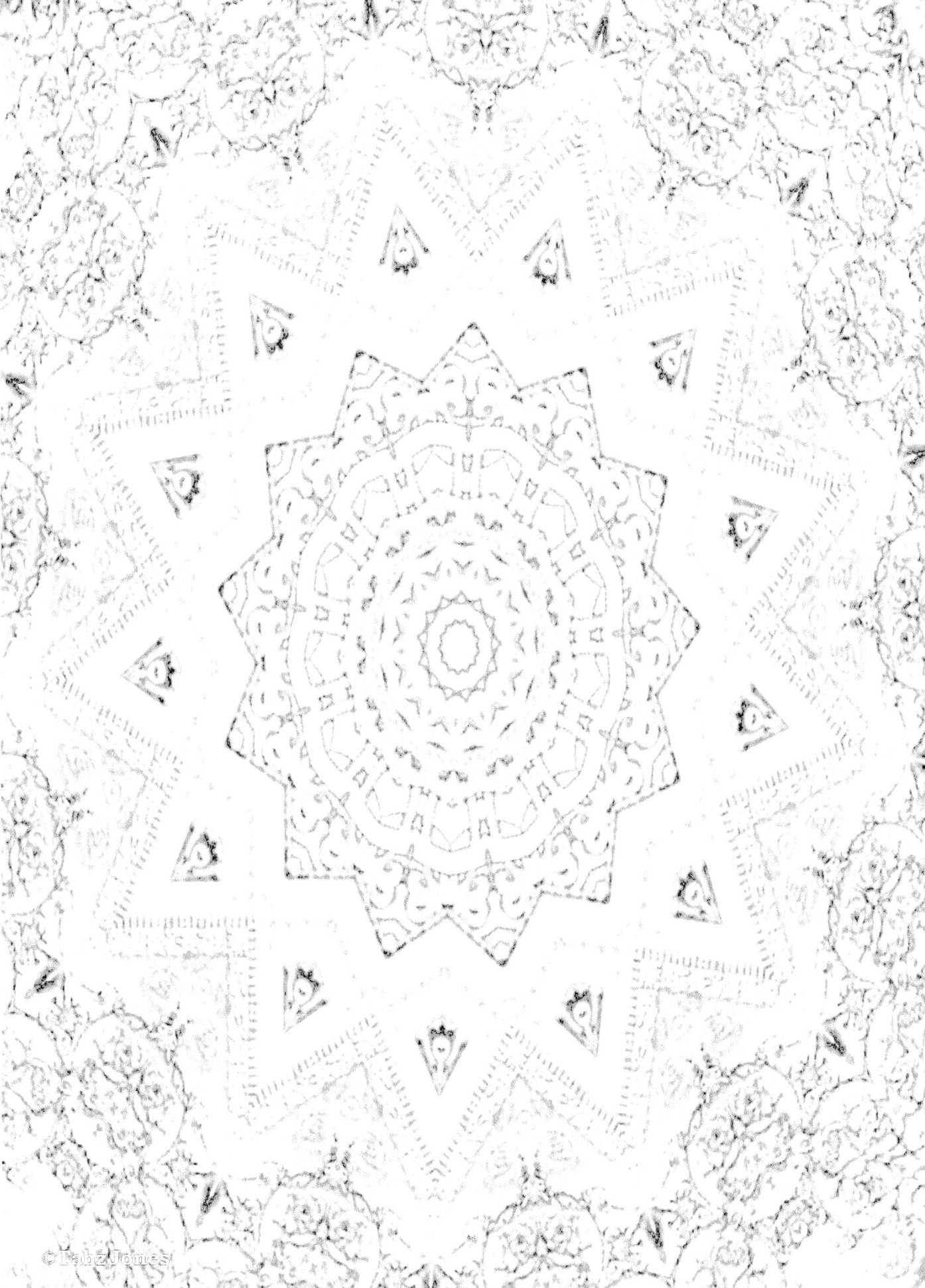

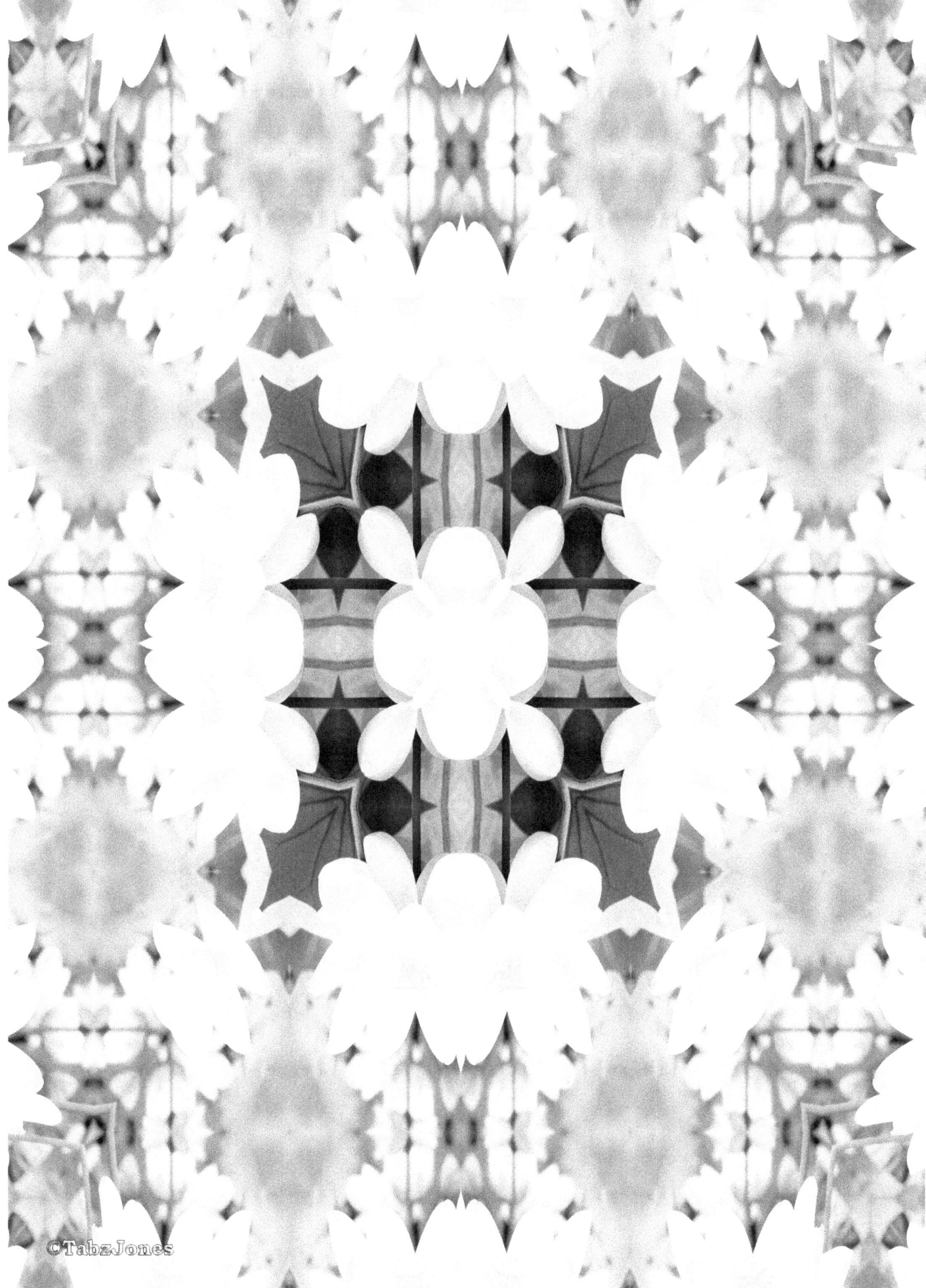

www.ingramcontent.com/pod-product-compliance
Lightning Source LLC
Chambersburg PA
CBHW081305180526
45170CB00007B/2577